A Family of Tortoises

Elvig Hansen

A & C Black · London

Contents

A & C Black (Publishers) Limited
35 Bedford Row, London WC1R 4JH
This edition © 1990 A & C Black (Publishers) Limited

Originally published in German under the title
'So lebt die Schildkrote' © 1989 by
Kinderbuchverlag KBV Luzern AG

Acknowledgements
The illustrations are by Helen Senior
Translated by Jane Sutton

ISBN 0 7136 3218 6

A CIP catalogue record for this book is available
from the British Library

Typeset by Method Ltd, Epping, Essex, UK
Printed in Belgium by Proost International Book Production

Introducing tortoises

Tortoises have lived on this planet for 180 million years. They have hardly altered in shape all this time. There are about 250 different species, including the terrapin family, the fresh-water turtle family and the sea turtles.

Until recently, thousands of tortoises were collected from the wild and sold as pets all over the world. A huge number of animals died, on the journey or because they were not looked after properly as pets. In the wild, tortoises have all the warmth they need, but in cold climates they cannot digest food properly, and their eggs do not hatch. The number of wild tortoises became dangerously low and some kinds were nearly extinct.

The import of tortoises is now banned, so tortoises can only rarely be kept as pets, and it is hoped that wild tortoises will increase. Unfortunately they are not protected in the wild and many are killed on the roads or destroyed as pests.

In this book we look at land tortoises, particularly the European spur-thighed tortoise, which lives in the southern Mediterranean countries, and countries as far away as Iran.

Finding wild tortoises

It is the beginning of March and in the Greek hills, spring has started. Even this early in the year it is hot: the thermometer already shows 22°C.

On a sunny grass slope, a tortoise appears, crawling around among the goats and sheep. The spring weather has woken it from hibernation.

The next day, a few more tortoises appear. After a week, there are twelve tortoises in the pasture. They have everything they need to live: plenty of sun, enough shade beneath stones, and lots of food.

Courtship and mating

A few days after the tortoises have woken from hibernation, when they have enough energy from lying in the sun, the mating season begins. Now the usually slow reptiles become very lively, and the males start to chase after the females.

When a male catches up with a female, he rams her with his shell and bites her legs over and over again. With powerful thrusts of his shell, he tries to corner her and make her stand still. Tortoises are usually silent, but at mating time the male becomes so excited he lets off loud squeaks.

The violent chase often lasts hours, but mating is over in a few minutes.

How to tell a male and female apart

You can only tell the difference between a male and a female tortoise if you turn them on their backs. The shell on the female's stomach (on the right) curves outwards, and she has a shorter tail. The male has a concave shell on his stomach, which makes it easier for him to mate with the female.

Courtship rivalry

If two equally strong males find they are chasing the same female, they will fight. These fights can go on for several hours – the two rivals bang at each other's shells until they are completely exhausted or until the weaker one runs away. In the mating season, there are tortoise fights going on over several weeks. When they stop it's a sign that all the females have mated.

Digging a nest

The females do not lay their eggs until two months after mating. In June they start to look for a suitable place. This female has found a sheltered place between some big clumps of grass.

It is nine o'clock in the morning and the temperature is 35°C. The female starts her strenuous task of digging a nest.

She scrapes up the hard dried-out soil with her powerful back legs and long claws. She keeps her balance with one back leg, while she digs about eight times with the other. Then she changes legs, and carries on.

An hour later, the tortoise has only managed to dig two centimetres deep. After half an hour, she reaches looser soil. Now her progress is quicker, and after another quarter of an hour the hole is five centimetres deep. She digs on tirelessly. It is now eleven o'clock. How much longer can she last in the heat?

Egg laying

Suddenly, the tortoise stops digging. She sits still for a moment, with her tail in the hole – and there is an egg. Immediately she scrapes some earth over it, then presses the soil down with her stomach shell. Finally she pulls some grass over the nest with her back legs.

The nest is well hidden and the tortoise disappears into the shade. She will not return to the egg.

As she crawls away, a flock of sheep comes past. Some of the animals trample over the place where the egg is buried. The vulnerable egg is broken.

Fortunately the tortoise lays more eggs. In total she will lay ten to twelve eggs each year, but she doesn't lay them all at once. She only has room in her body for three to five eggs at most.

The female tortoise digs a new hole for each clutch. Each egg weighs twenty grams and is about four centimetres long. The pictures below show their actual size. Each one has a hard chalky shell like a hen's egg.

Thieves feed on the eggs

The eggs are food for lots of animals. The female tortoise lays her eggs in several different places so that thieves don't find all the nests. Hedgehogs are egg thieves, as are squirrels, rats, foxes, martens and polecats. They sniff out the hiding places and dig up the eggs, so many eggs disappear soon after being laid. Perhaps only two nests out of ten will be well enough hidden to escape the hungry predators. Often, you can find twelve or so plundered nests in a small space of only thirty metres.

The eggs hatch

If the eggs are kept warm by the sun, it takes about ten weeks until they hatch. When the little tortoise is ready to hatch, it chips away at the egg shell with its egg-tooth, which is a sharp horny callous on its upper jaw. The egg-tooth is only used once and soon afterwards it drops off.

The young tortoise climbs out of the nest

Hatching out of the egg is hard work, but now the young tortoise must also dig itself out of the earth. This can take it quite a long time.

If there is a long cool period during the summer, followed by sunshine, the tortoises think it's spring and mate a second time. The female tortoises lay their eggs two months later, when it is almost autumn and too cold for the embryo to develop in the egg. But the tiny embryos do not die. They hibernate in the egg until the weather is warmer. By the beginning of summer they are ready to hatch.

The newly hatched tortoise explores

As soon as the tiny tortoise has reached the surface, it starts to explore. The newly hatched tortoise is very vulnerable. It is about four centimetres long and weighs just 20 grams. It is easy prey for rats, birds and other predators. It can't move quickly and it has no hole to hide in.

Even the young tortoise's shell doesn't offer any protection, as it is still soft. Hungry enemies are not the only danger – passing sheep and goats can also be dangerous. Their hooves are exactly the same size as the tiny tortoise. With just one step they can damage or kill the little animal.

Looking at the shell

In the picture above, you can see an adult tortoise which must have had an accident when it was small. There is a long crack in its shell which will have happened when the shell was still soft. When the shell hardened, the crack remained.

In adults, the shell is about three millimetres thick on the stomach and back, and about five millimetres thick at the sides. The shell can take a great deal of pressure without being damaged.

If a tortoise feels threatened, it tucks its head into its shell and blocks the front with its strong scaly legs.

Tortoises are cold-blooded

The morning sun has woken this tortoise. Cold and stiff, it crawls slowly out of its hole. Like all reptiles, tortoises are cold-blooded. When they wake up, the first thing tortoises need to do is sunbathe. After about an hour, when they have stored up enough heat, they can start to eat. Tortoises can only digest their food when their body temperature is around 30°C.

Feeding

The tortoise on the right is looking for flowers to eat. It takes a while to sniff them, then it picks off a tasty mouthful. Using its excellent sense of smell, it discovers some of its favourite food, clover. If there is a snail on one of the flowers, the tortoise eats that as well. It will also eat worms and insects.

Tortoises do not have teeth. Instead their jaws have powerful sharp edges. The tortoise tears off leaves with its horny jaws then swallows them whole without chewing them. The tortoise cannot stay in the sun for long. If it gets hotter than 38°C it will die of heatstroke. When the weather gets too hot, the tortoise hides in the shade until later.

This young tortoise only takes ten minutes to warm up in the morning because its shell is just a millimetre thick. It isn't yet strong enough to bite off leaves like the adults do. It uses its front legs to help: it bites into a leaf, grabbing with its front legs and pulling it to the ground. Then it pulls its head back into its shell until a small piece of the leaf breaks off.

The little tortoise can pull a leaf so hard that it will almost topple over. If the leaf is too high up, the tortoise tramples down the stalk until it can reach. After five clover leaves, the baby tortoise has eaten enough. It stays in the sun another half an hour to digest the food, then looks for a shady place to rest.

Droppings

Once a day, the tortoise leaves a small pile of droppings in the grass. A couple of dung beetles arrive, attracted by the smell. They bite off a piece and make it into a round ball with their back legs. Then they roll the ball away, bury it, and the female lays her eggs in it. When the larvae have hatched, they eat the ball of tortoise droppings.

Territories

Wild tortoises are well adapted to their surroundings. With their powerful legs and claws, they can move almost anywhere in the dry stony landscape. Although they live on land, they occasionally like to take a bath and have a long drink.

Tortoises don't move very fast or very far. In the wild, they each have a territory of about 30 metres square. If you move one of these tortoises even a hundred metres from its territory, it immediately sets off back again using its sense of smell to find its way.

Falling over

As the tortoise crawls between rocks and stones, it can easily fall onto its back. Then it must get back on its feet as quickly as possible.

First of all it lies quite quietly. Then it starts to thrash around with all four legs to try to get a firm hold with its claws. If it manages, it's soon back on its stomach again.

If not, the tortoise has to try again. It suddenly waggles its head to and fro very quickly about six times which turns it over a little way. Then it starts thrashing with its front legs. This time it's lucky – it catches hold of a dry tuft of grass with its back claws and pulls itself onto its stomach.

The tortoise rests for a little while after its exhausting efforts, then crawls away as if nothing has happened.

A healthy tortoise can nearly always get back onto its feet. But a sick or weak tortoise may not have the strength. If it cannot recover itself, it will die, baked in its own shell by the sun.

Enemies

Tortoises have many enemies. Soft baby tortoises may be eaten by ravens, crows and magpies, so they spend most of the time hiding in long grass where they will be well camouflaged. But here they are easy prey for another predator, the snake.

Adult tortoises are protected by their shells. Dogs and foxes may try to see if there is something there, but they are unlikely to be able to reach into the shell and find the soft parts.

The golden eagle is more successful. It carries the tortoise in its claws high into the air, then drops it on a rock. The shell shatters and the eagle has its meal.

Parasites

Parasites don't usually kill the animals they feed on, but they can make them ill and weak. The tortoise can get blood-sucking ticks. The tick cannot lay its eggs until it has drunk plenty of blood. When the tick in the top picture has filled itself with the tortoise's blood, it will fall off and lay its eggs in the ground.

A tortoise has soft skin just at the place where its back legs come out of the shell. This is where the ticks can bite easily. The tortoise in the bottom picture has lots of these tormentors.

How to tell the age of a tortoise

A tortoise never grows too big for its shell: they both grow together. The shell is made of lots of large plates. On the outside they are made of horn, which contains the colours and the pattern. On the inside they are made of bone, which is part of the tortoise's skeleton.

As the tortoise grows, the horny plates grow thicker and bigger, and develop age rings. From these, you can roughly tell how old a tortoise is. In the top picture you can see a tortoise that's not quite a year old – the horn plates only have one ring.

In the lower picture you can see the horn plate of an older animal, which has between 15 and 20 rings. This tortoise is at least 20 years old. It will not grow any more and no further rings will develop. The old rings will become more and more worn out.

When a tortoise is over 20, it's no longer possible to tell its age accurately, but we know that they can be very old: some live to be over a hundred.

Giant tortoises

Tortoises belong to a very old group in the animal kingdom. From fossilized remains, we can tell that prehistoric tortoises looked very like the present day ones. At that time the large kinds lived in Australia and India, and grew up to three metres long.

Today there are only a few large tortoises. The Giant Galapagos tortoise (or elephant tortoise) lives only on the tiny Galapagos islands off the coast of South America. Its shell can be over a metre long and a metre high. A fully grown giant tortoise can weigh up to 300 kilograms. By the time it weighs this much, it may be nearly 200 years old.

There used to be over 200,000 of these giants in the Galapagos islands. But they were hunted for their meat and now there are only about 15,000 left. Like many kinds of tortoise, they are now strictly protected and are not allowed to be caught or killed.

Hibernation

Back in Greece, it is now the middle of November. The hot summer days are over and winter is approaching. It is cold now, and the tortoises can no longer digest their food, so it's time for them to hibernate.

This tortoise has found a place to hibernate among some dead plants. It digs a hole deep in the ground where it will be protected from the frost.

Here it will sleep for four or five months, and won't wake up again until March when the spring sun warms the earth. Then the tortoise's life will start again.

Index